AF897189

Alfred's

Basic Graded Piano Course

Theory Book

Preparatory

This Alfred's Basic Graded Piano Course Theory Book was written in response to many requests from teachers for an Alfred Course that enables students to pass the graded exams that are so much a part of the learning experience throughout the world. It uses the Lesson Book to introduce sight-reading and technique, as well as preparation for pieces, alongside this correlated Theory Book to prepare for the Theory exam.

By including examples from previous papers and a mock theory paper that the student might expect to see in the exam, you, as a teacher can judge perfectly the appropriate time to enter your pupil for the graded exam. This will make passing a formality and, more importantly, give your pupil the confidence to achieve the merits and distinctions that inspire and reward their hard work.

Assign with Lesson Book p.2

Writing Semitones

SEMITONES • NO KEY BETWEEN

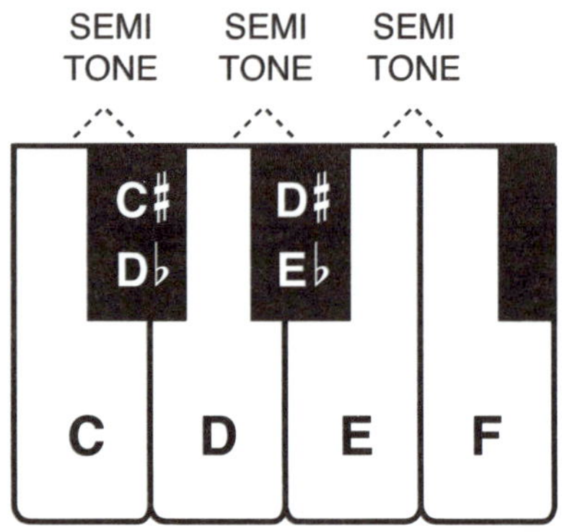

A **SEMITONE** is the distance from any key to the very next key above or below, whether black or white.

The SHARP sign ♯ raises a note a semitone (play next key to the right).
The FLAT sign ♭ lowers a note a semitone (play next key to the left).
The NATURAL sign ♮ cancels a sharp or flat!

Each black key may be named 2 ways.

EXAMPLE: C♯ = D♭

These white keys may also be named 2 ways.

EXAMPLE: C = B♯ F = E♯ B = C♭ E = F♭

2. Write 2 different names for each indicated key, as shown in the first 2 examples:

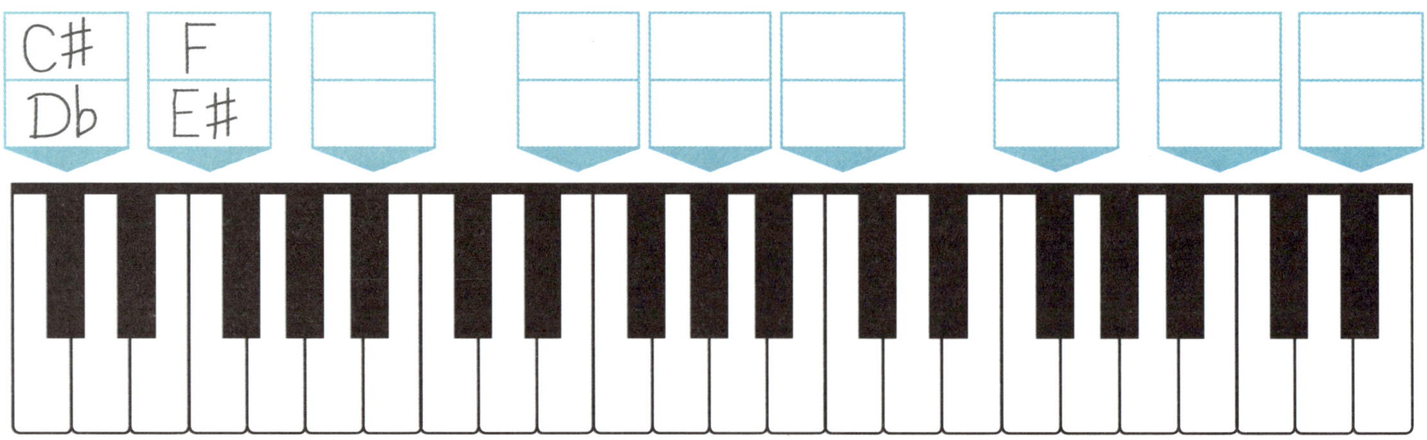

Writing Whole Tones

A **WHOLE TONE** is equal to 2 semitones.
Skip one key... black or white.

WHOLE TONES • ONE KEY BETWEEN

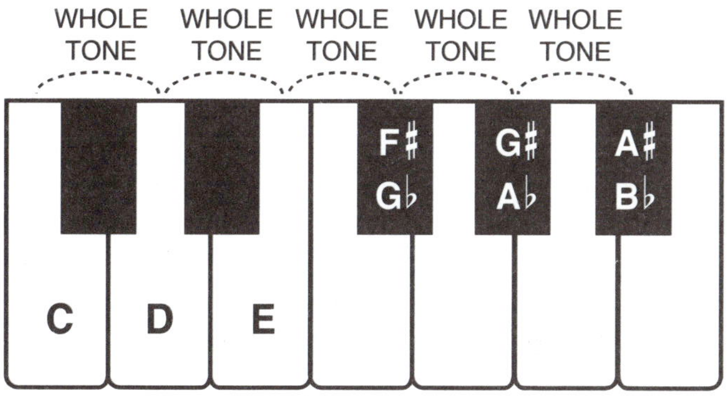

1. Write the names on the keys, continuing up the keyboard in WHOLE TONES.
   Use SHARPS for the black keys.

2. Write the names on the keys, continuing up the keyboard in WHOLE TONES.
   Use FLATS for the black keys.

3. In the following squares write ½ for each SEMITONE and 1 for each WHOLE TONE indicated by the arrows.

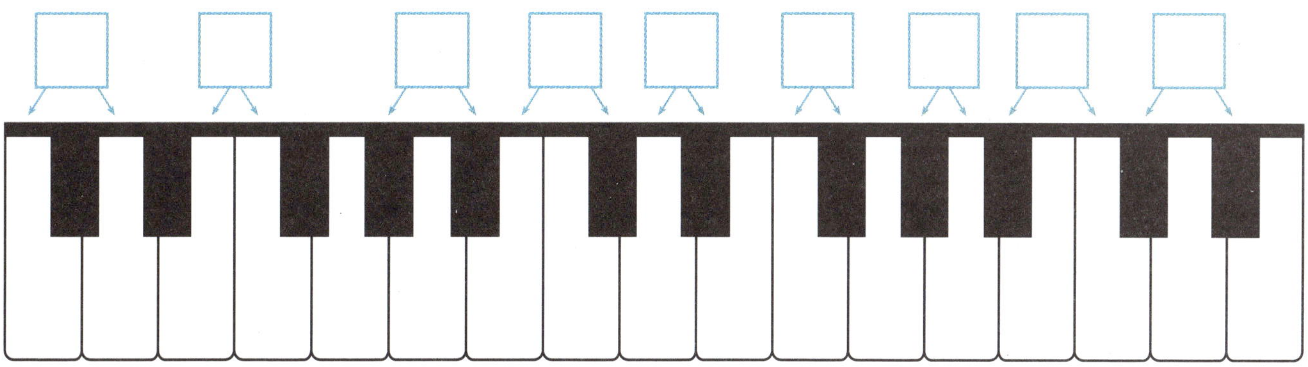

Assign with Lesson Book p.8

Tetrachords

A **TETRACHORD** is a series of **FOUR NOTES** having a pattern of:

WHOLE TONE, WHOLE TONE, SEMITONE

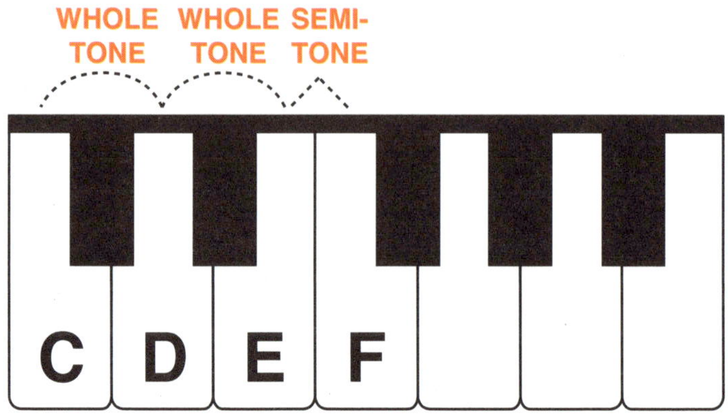

The four notes of a tetrachord must always be **NEIGHBOURING LETTERS** of the **MUSICAL ALPHABET.**

1. Study the TETRACHORDS on the keyboards below and answer these questions:
   - Does each consist of WHOLE TONE, WHOLE TONE, SEMITONE?
   - Are the notes of each tetrachord NEIGHBOURING LETTERS of the musical alphabet?
   - Underline the correct spelling of the **D** tetrachord: **D E G♭ G** **D E F♯ G**
   - Underline the correct spelling of the **A** tetrachord: **A B D♭ D** **A B C♯ D**

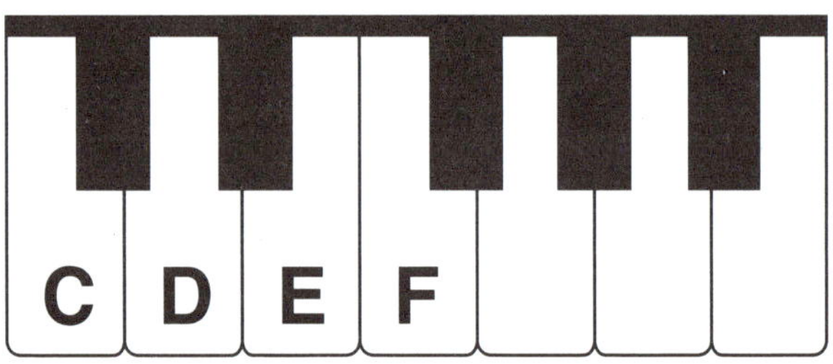

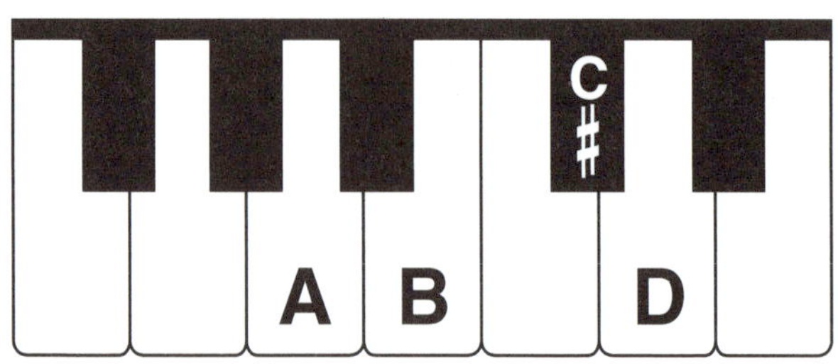

2. Write tetrachords beginning on each of the following notes:

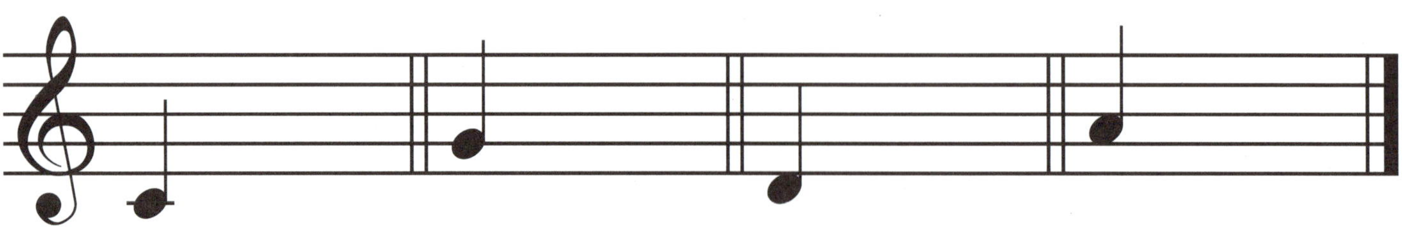

Writing the Major Scale

1. Write the letter names of the notes of the C MAJOR SCALE on the keyboard below.
2. Play the 1st tetrachord with LH 5 4 3 2, and the 2nd tetrachord with RH 2 3 4 5.

THE C MAJOR SCALE

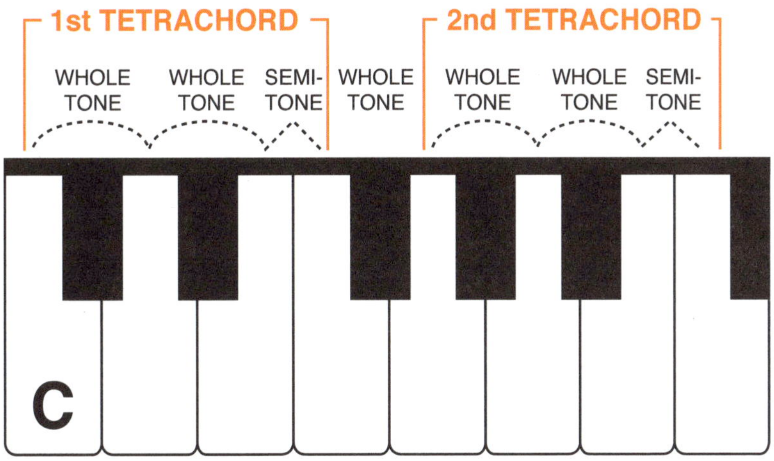

3. Write the letter names of the notes of the G MAJOR SCALE on the keyboard below.
4. Play the 1st tetrachord with LH 5 4 3 2, and the 2nd tetrachord with RH 2 3 4 5.

THE G MAJOR SCALE

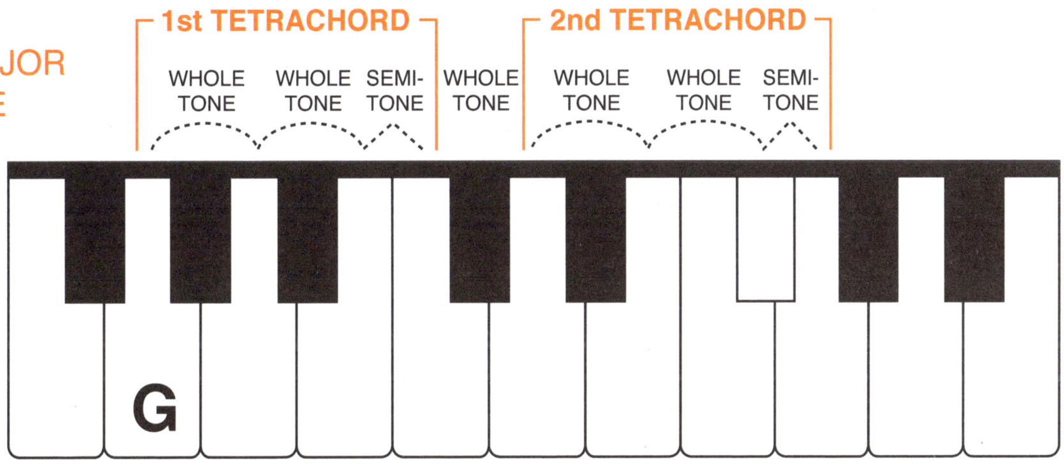

5. Write tetrachords beginning on each of the following notes.
6. Play as follows: 1st tetrachord with LH 5 4 3 2, 2nd with RH 2 3 4 5.
   2nd tetrachord with LH 5 4 3 2, 3rd with RH 2 3 4 5.
   3rd tetrachord with LH 5 4 3 2, 4th with RH 2 3 4 5.

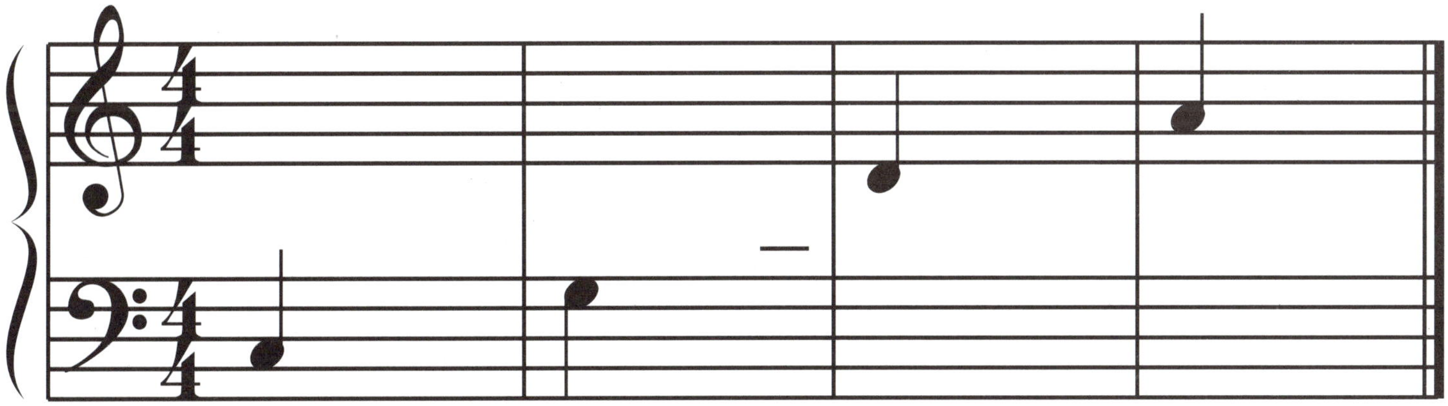

Assign with Lesson Book p.14

Music with 2 RH Positions

LH & RH in C POSITION

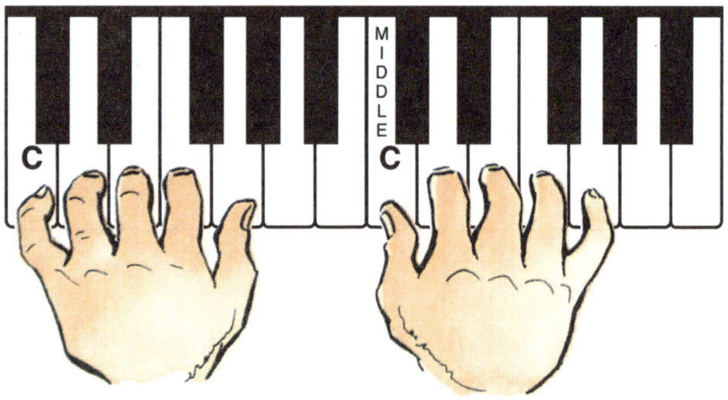

LH in C POSITION **RH in G POSITION**

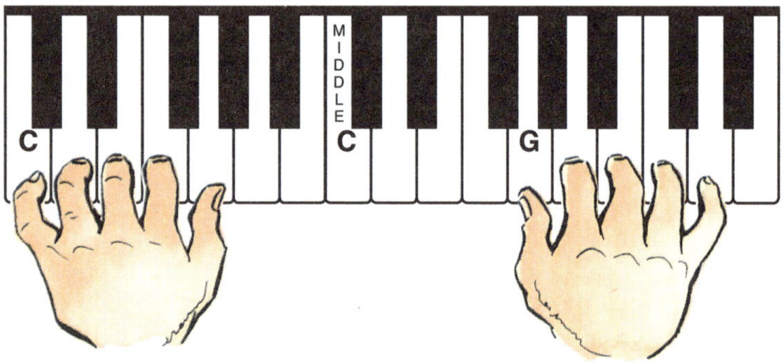

1. Write the name of the key played by each RH finger in C POSITION:

KEY					
RH FINGER	1	2	3	4	5

2. Write the name of the key played by each LH finger in C POSITION:

KEY					
LH FINGER	5	4	3	2	1

3. Write the name of the key played by each RH finger in G POSITION:

KEY					
RH FINGER	1	2	3	4	5

The Fox

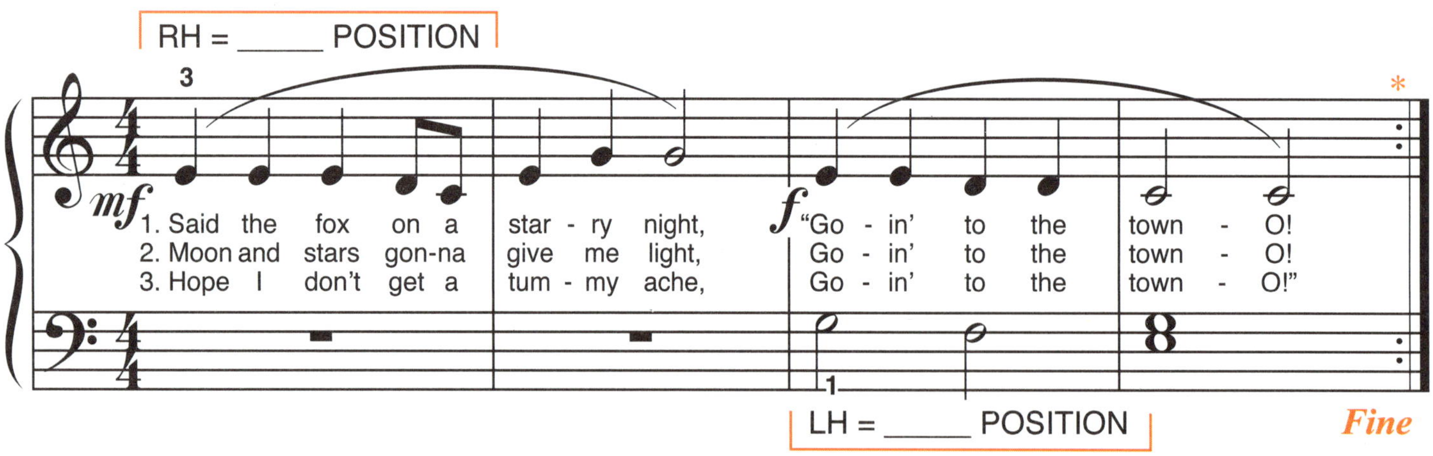

Music with 2 LH Positions

1. Write the name of the key played by each LH finger in G POSITION:

KEY					
LH FINGER	5	4	3	2	1

2. Write the name of the key played by each RH finger in G POSITION:

KEY					
RH FINGER	1	2	3	4	5

3. Write the name of the key played by each LH finger in C POSITION:

KEY					
LH FINGER	5	4	3	2	1

LH & RH in G POSITION

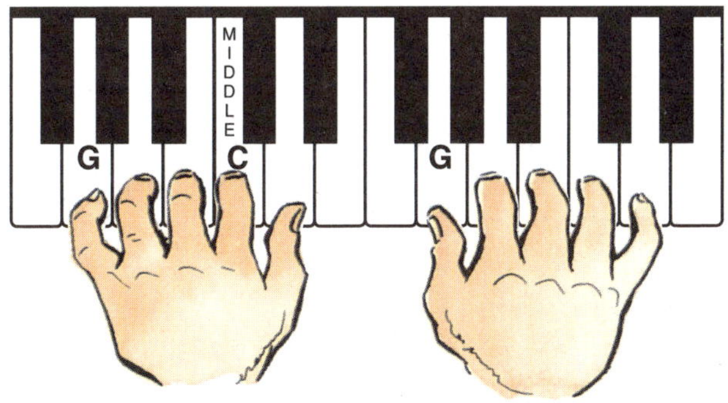

LH in C POSITION **RH in G POSITION**

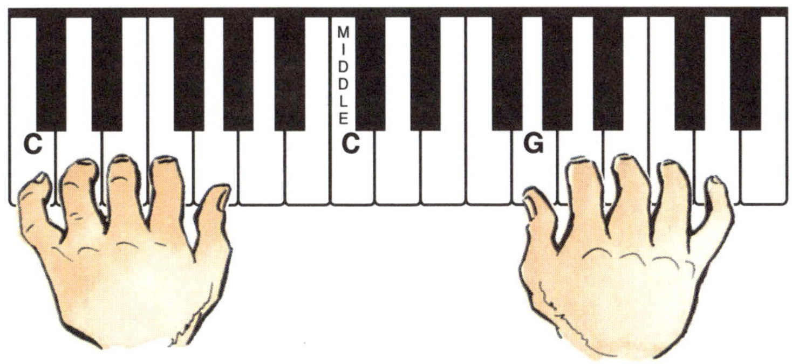

A Merry Song

KEY OF C MAJOR
Key Signature: no ♯, no ♭

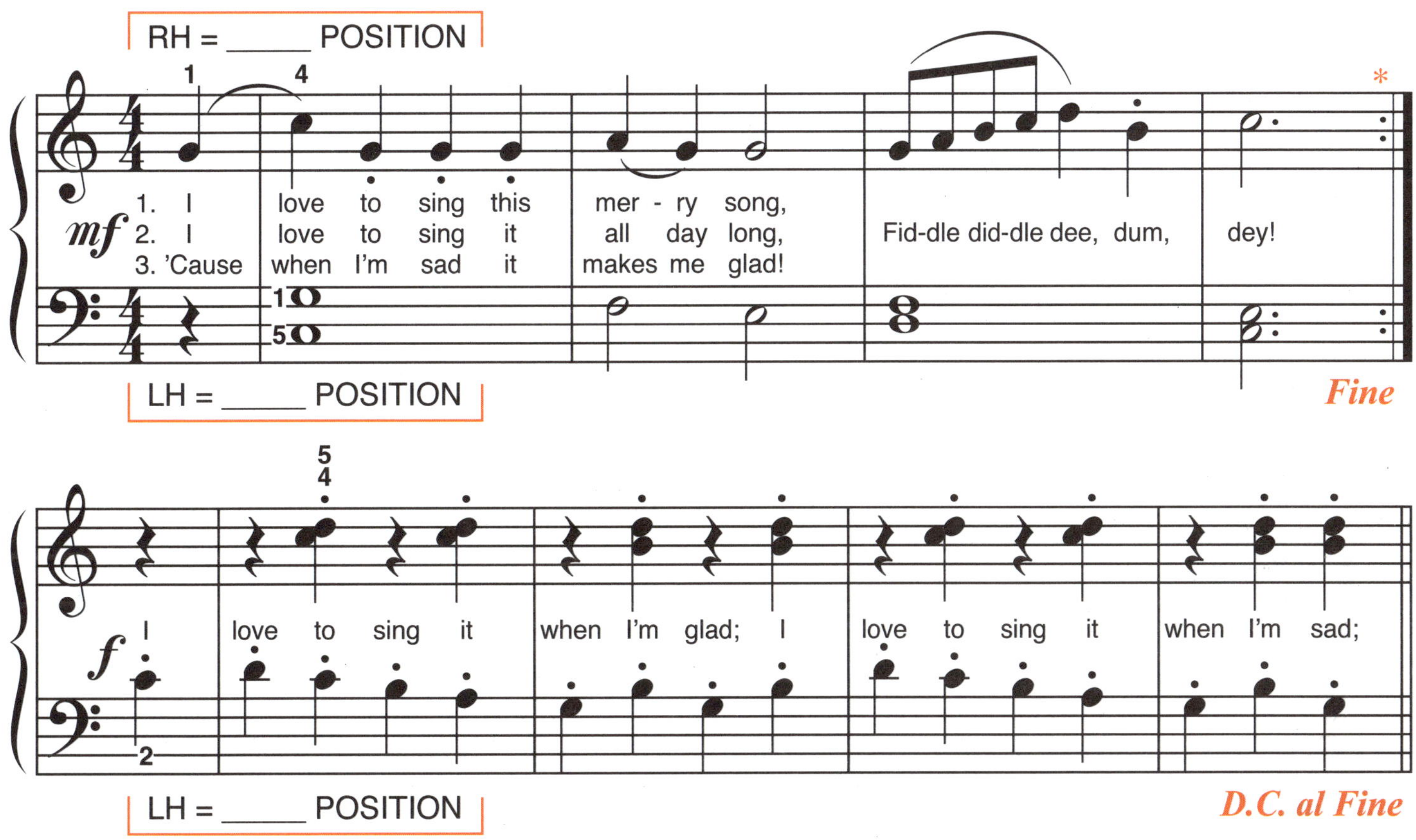

Identify the U.F.O.s!

The U.F.O.'s (Unidentified Flying Objects) on pages 7 and 8 can be changed to I.F.O.'s (Identified Flying Objects)!

To change the U.F.O.'s to I.F.O.'s, print the names of each space ship on the tag attached to it. Select from the following names:

CROTCHET REST	SHARP	FORTE	TIED NOTES	TIME SIGNATURE
MINIM REST	FLAT	MEZZO FORTE	ACCENT	REPEAT
SEMIBREVE REST	NATURAL	PIANO	PAUSE	QUAVERS

SCORE 100 FOR EACH U.F.O. YOU IDENTIFY! PERFECT SCORE IS 1,500!

Assign with Lesson Book p.18

FOR BONUS SCORE, ANSWER THE FOLLOWING QUESTIONS
TO MAKE 1,700 AND QUALIFY AS A SUPER-STUDENT!

1. ***p–f*** means ______________________________.

2. [decrescendo sign] means "gradually ______________________________."

FINAL SCORE: ______________________

Assign with Lesson Book p.21

Dotted Crotchets in $\frac{3}{4}$ Time

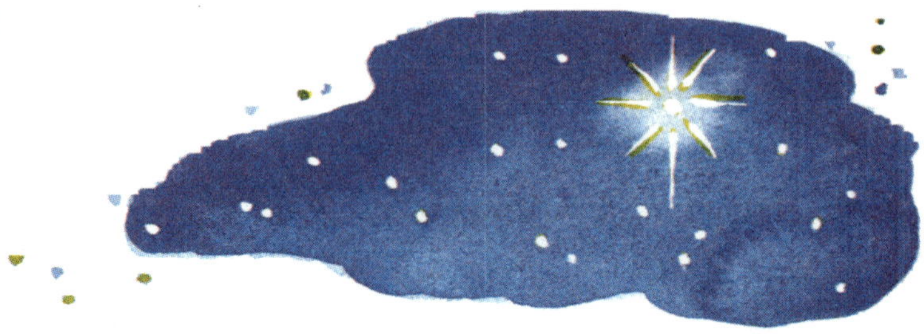

1. In the following line, draw TIES as indicated.
2. Play and count.
3. Play and sing the words.

4. In the following line, some crotchets need dots.
   Add the correct dots to make the rhythm the same as above.
5. Play and count. This line should sound *exactly* the same as the one above.

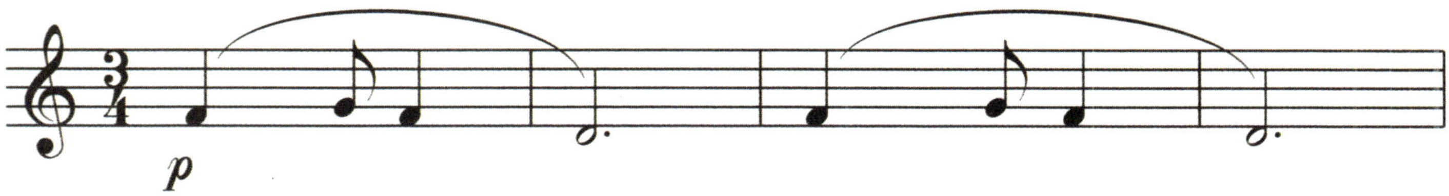

Dotted Crotchets in $\frac{4}{4}$ Time

1. In the following line, draw TIES as indicated.
2. Play and count.
3. Play and sing the words.

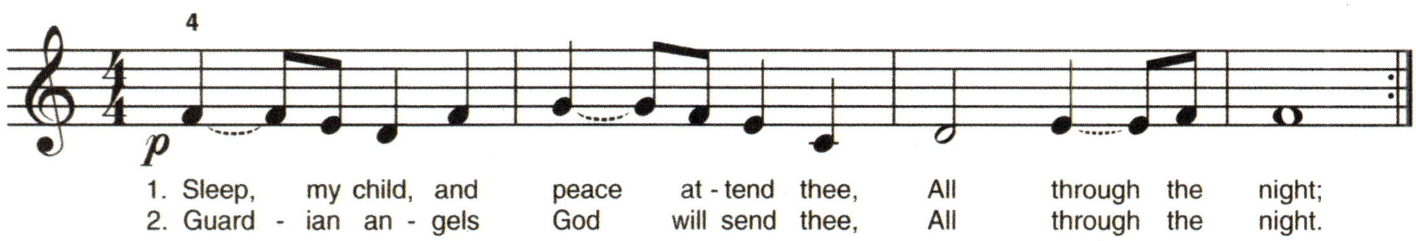

4. In the following line, there are some dots missing from crotchets and some tails missing from quavers. Add everything that is needed to make the rhythm the same as above.
5. Play and count. This line should sound *exactly* the same as the one above.

Assign with Lesson Book p.24

Writing 6ths

REMEMBER: 6ths are written LINE-SPACE or SPACE-LINE

1. Write the name of each note in the following boxes.
2. Play these MELODIC INTERVALS, saying "Up a 6th," etc.

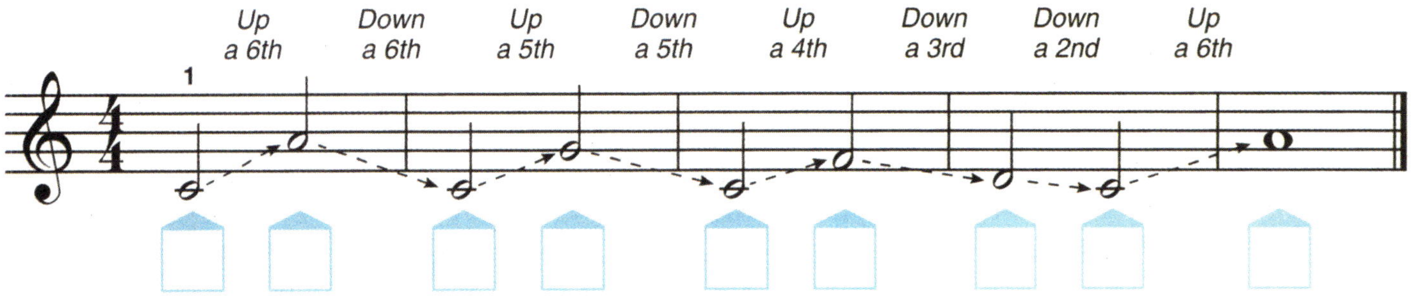

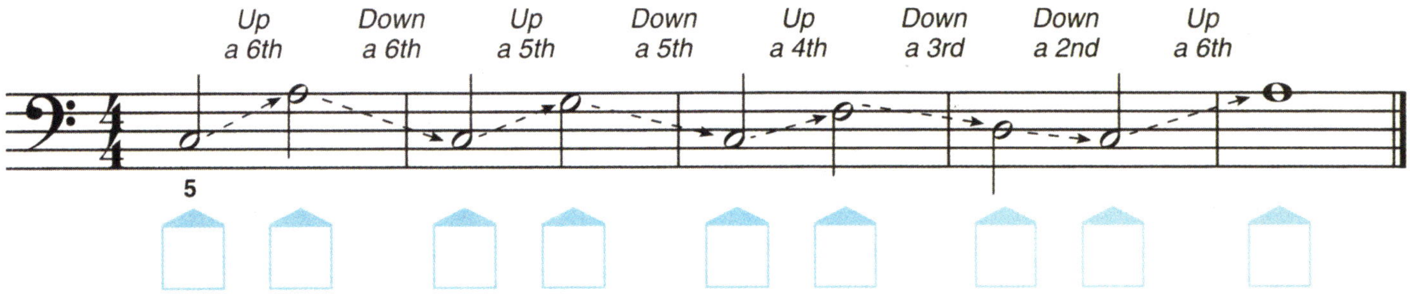

3. In each bar below, add a higher semibreve to make the indicated HARMONIC INTERVAL.

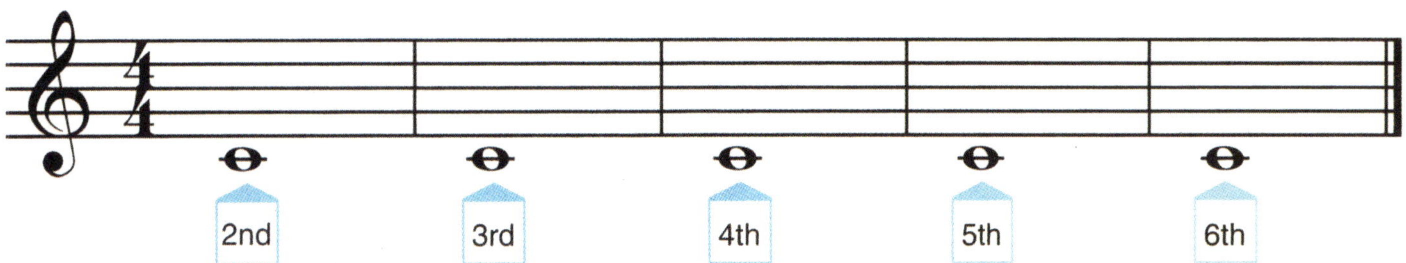

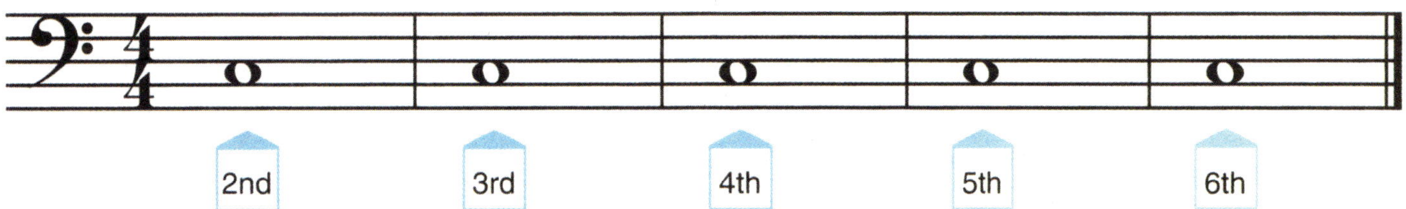

4. Play the above two lines. Use RH 1–5 or LH 5–1 on each 5th and 6th.

Assign with Lesson Book p.24

Interval Search

Draw a flight path from each beehive to the flower that contains the interval of the same name. The paths may cross, but may not pass through a different interval! (There will be two bees from each beehive.)

Score 10 for each interval found.

PERFECT SCORE = 100

YOUR SCORE ________

Writing 6ths in G Position

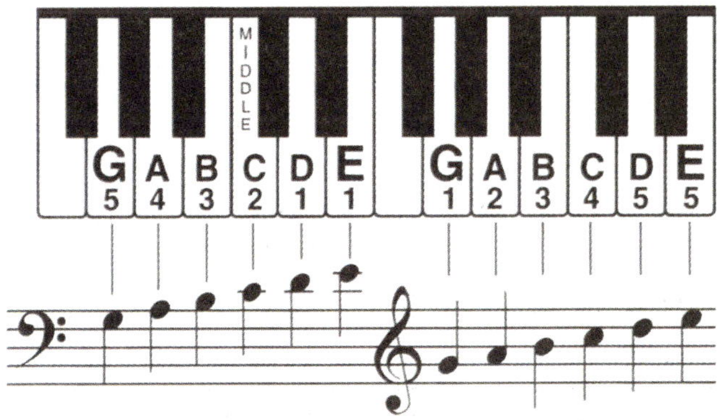

1. In each bar below, add one higher semibreve to make the indicated HARMONIC interval.
2. Play. Use RH 1-5 on the 5th and the 6th.

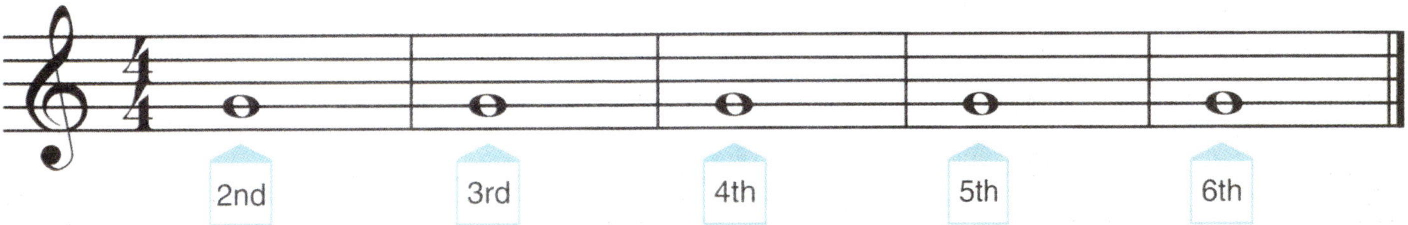

3. In each bar below, add one higher semibreve to make the indicated HARMONIC interval.
4. Play. Use LH 5-1 on the 5th and the 6th.

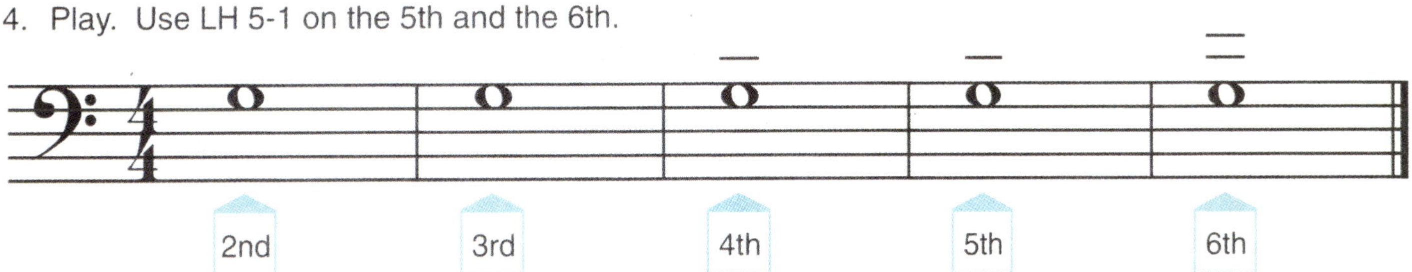

5. Write the name of each note in the following boxes.
6. Play, saying "Down a 4th," etc.

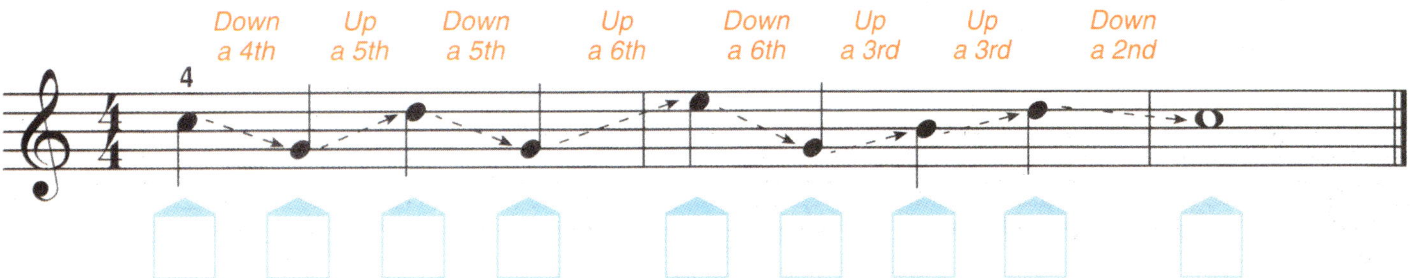

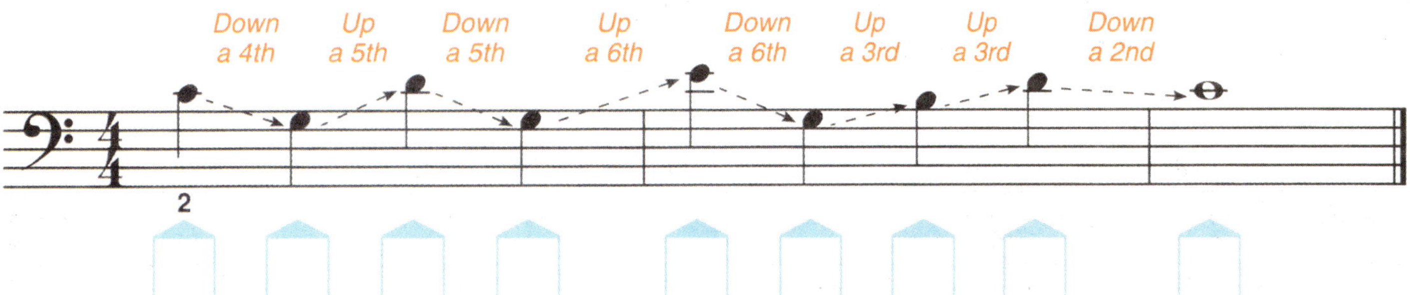

7. What kind of intervals (harmonic or melodic) did you play in the last 2 lines?____________________

Assign with Lesson Book p.32

Writing 6ths Up & Down the Keyboard

1. Add a note a 6th ABOVE each of the following notes.
   Say the name of the note as you write it.
2. Play, using RH 1–5 on each 6th.

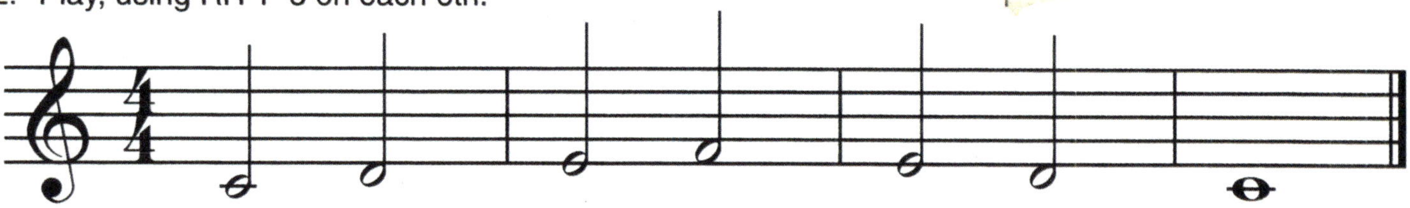

3. Add a note a 6th BELOW each of the following notes.
   Say the name of the note as you write it.
4. Play, using LH 5–1 on each 6th.

5. Play the two lines as one complete piece—play RH, then LH.

Writing 6ths Around the Keyboard

1. Add a note a 6th ABOVE each of the following notes.
   Say the name of the note as you write it.
2. Play, using RH 1–5 on each 6th.

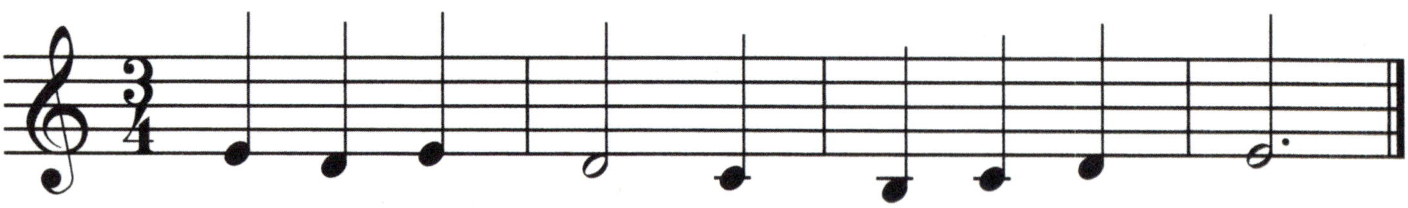

3. Add a note a 6th BELOW each of the following notes.
   Say the name of the note as you write it.
4. Play, using LH 5–1 on each 6th.

5. Play the two lines as one complete piece—play RH, then LH.

Interval Review

1. Write a note higher than the given note to form the melodic interval specified (like the example):

2. Write a note higher than the given note to form the harmonic interval specified (like the example):

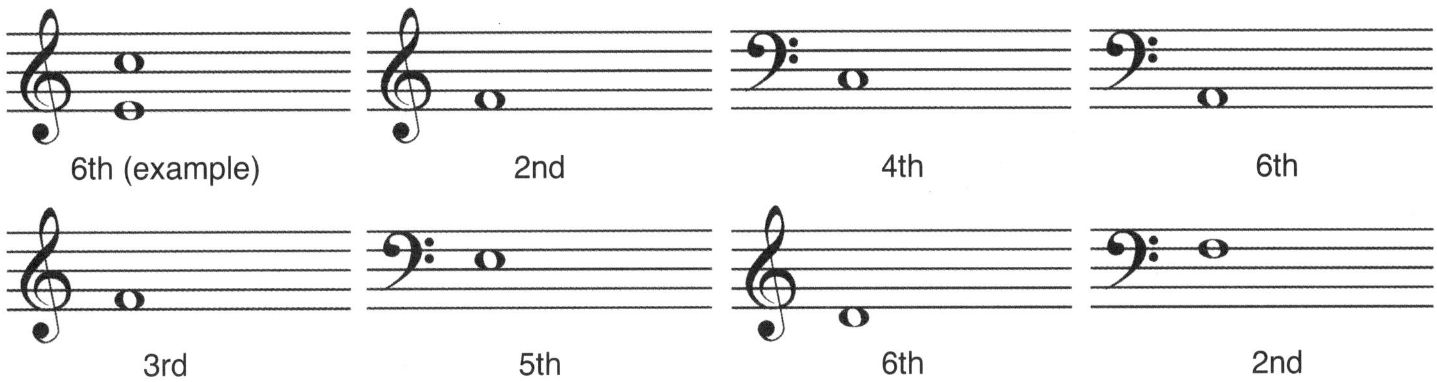

3. Circle two notes a sixth apart in this melody:

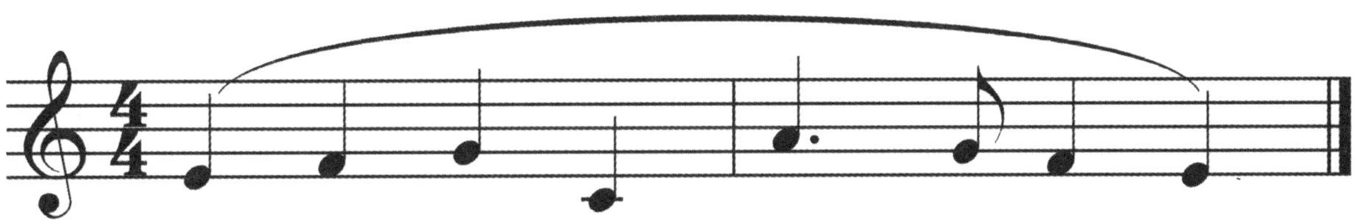

4. Circle two notes a third apart in this melody:

Assign with Lesson Book p.34

General Exercises

Look at the melody below and answer the questions that follow:

1. Time Names and Values:

i) What is the time value of the shortest note? __________

ii) What is the time value of the longest note? __________

iii) Which bar has no crotchets? __________

iv) Which bar has only quavers? __________

2. Note Names

i) Name the highest note. __________

ii) Name the lowest note. __________

iii) Can you identify the note that occurs most often? __________

iv) What note does the piece end on? __________

3. Time Signatures

i) What does the 3 in $\frac{3}{4}$ mean? __________

ii) What does the 4 in $\frac{3}{4}$ mean? __________

4. Rhythms

i) How many times does the rhythm 𝅗𝅥 ♩ occur? __________

ii) Complete this sentence:

Bar 2 has the same rhythm as bar __________

5. Dynamics

i) Which of the following describes the dynamics of the piece?

a) Getting louder
b) Getting softer
c) Starting soft, getting louder then finishing softly
d) Starting loud and getting gradually softer

____

Crossing LH 2 over 1

You can play any 6 neighbouring white keys in a row, going UP the keyboard with the LH, by starting with the 5th finger and crossing 2 over 1.

1. Write the finger number under each of the following notes, as shown in the first example.
2. Write the names of the notes in the boxes.
3. Play.

Assign with Lesson Book p.38

Crossing RH 2 over 1

You can also play any 6 neighbouring white keys in a row, coming DOWN the keyboard with the RH, by starting with the 5th finger and crossing 2 over 1.

1. Write the finger number under each of the following notes, as shown in the first example.
2. Write the names of the notes in the boxes.
3. Play.

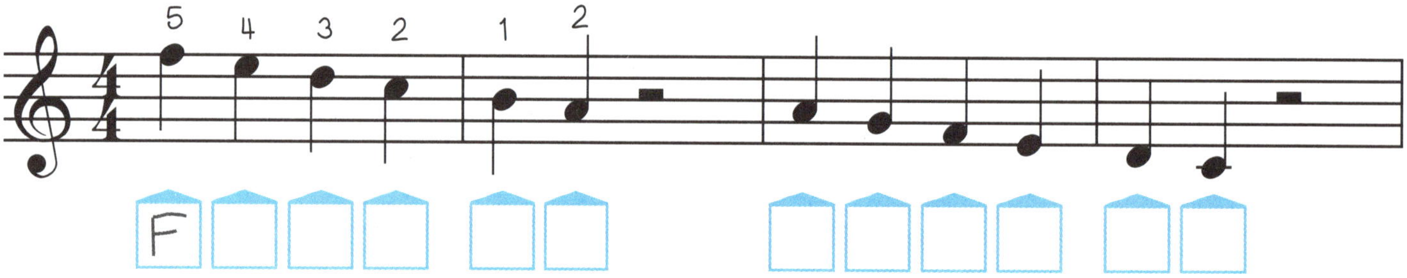

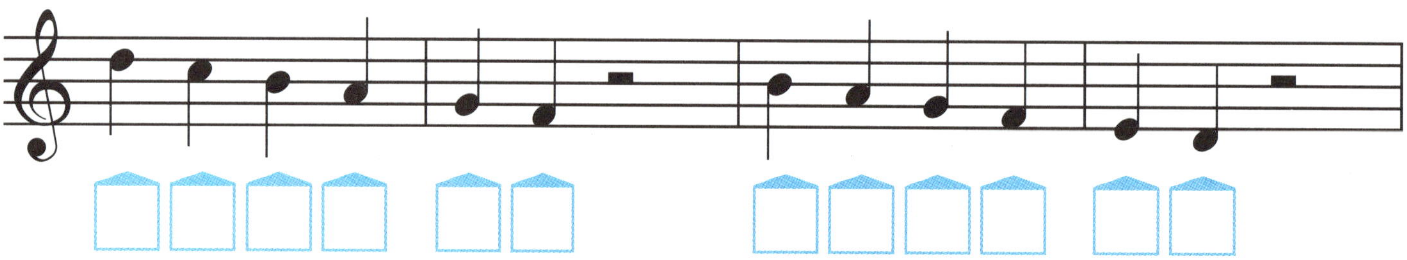

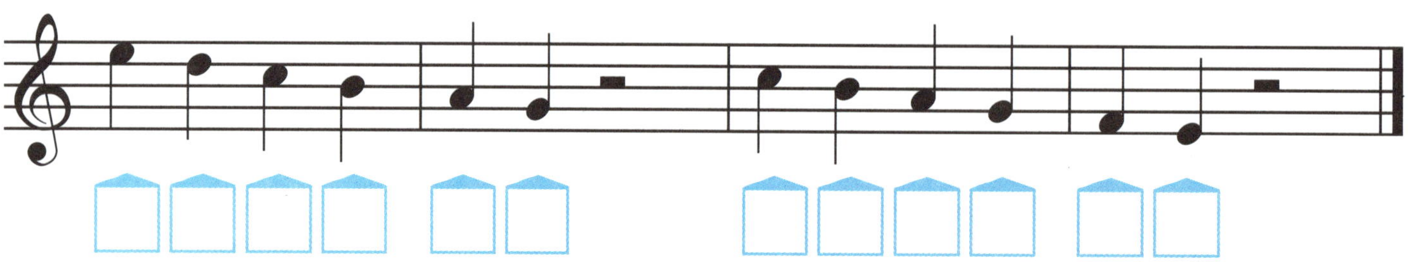

Assign with Lesson Book p.40

Note Grouping

Beaming notes is usually done in crotchet (quarter note) beats for simple time signatures.

For 2/4 and 3/4 time signatures, quavers (eighth notes) can be beamed as whole bars:

Unbeamed:

Beamed:

3/4 beaming in four quavers:

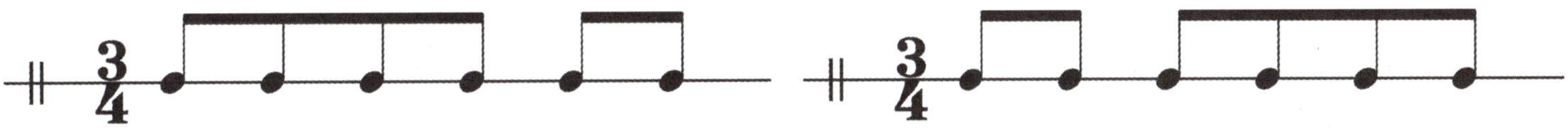

3/4 beaming in crotchet beats (three groups of two quavers):

In 4/4, beam quavers across beats 1 and 2, or 3 and 4, **but NEVER between 2 and 3.**

Unbeamed:

Beamed:

Complete the following bars with groupings of quavers (eighth notes):

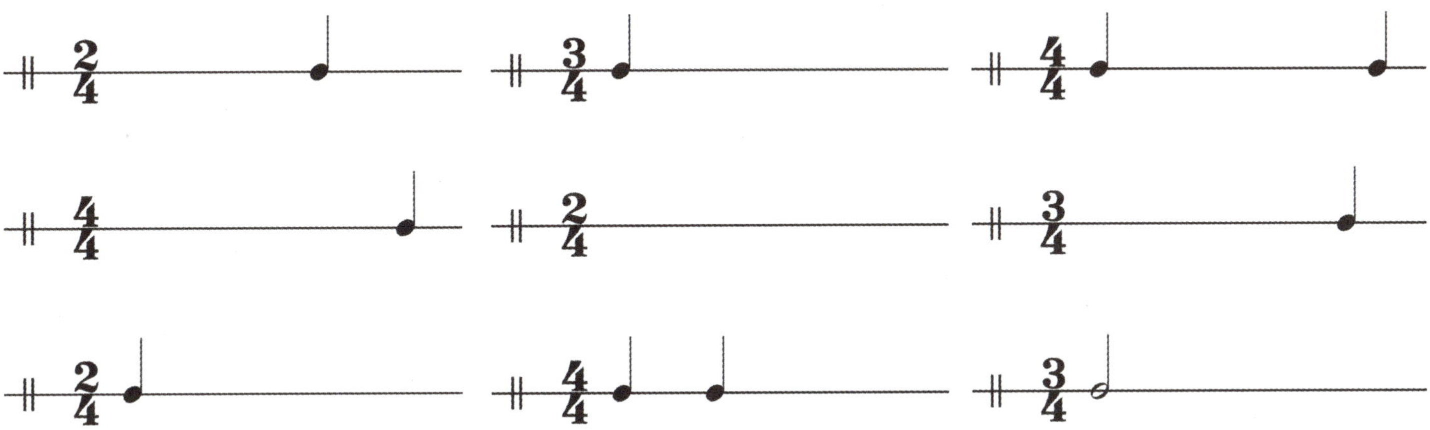

Assign with Lesson Book p.43

Composing an Answering Rhythm

4 bar rhythms usually use a 2 bar question and a 2 bar answer. Each bar is given a letter name so repeated rhythms can be indicated by the same letter name like: ABAC; ABBC; ABCB; this shows the patterns of repetition and contrast.

1. Give each rhythm pattern a letter name as in example A:

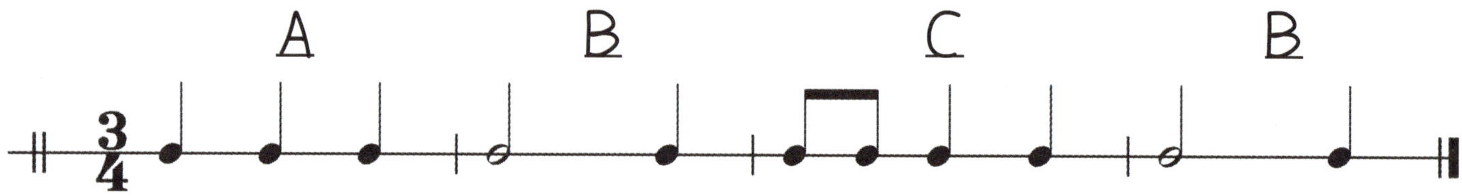

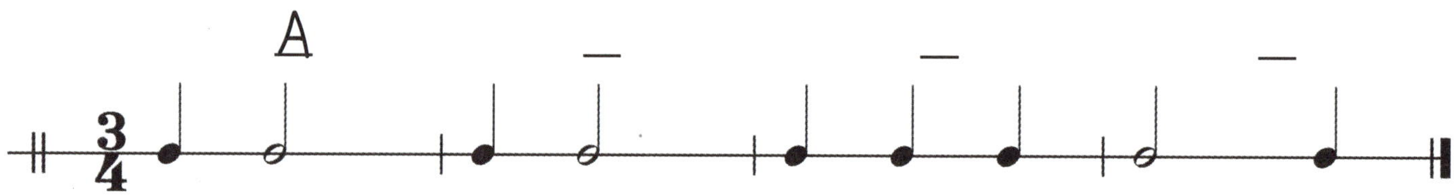

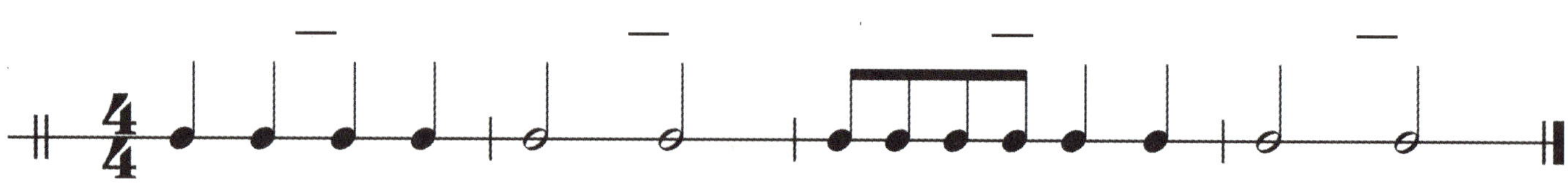

2. Answer the 2 bar rhythm patterns using the letter names indicated:

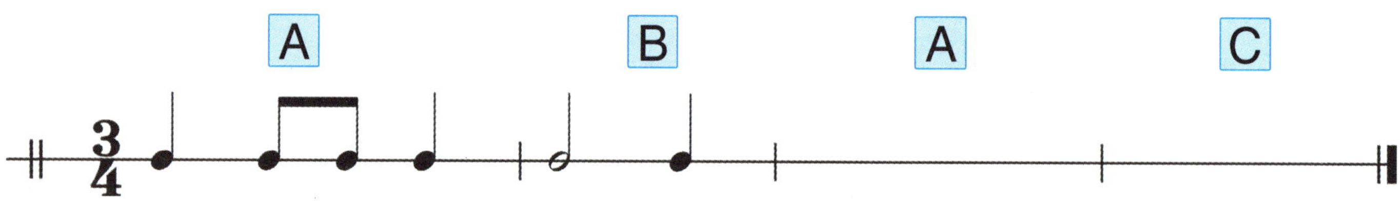

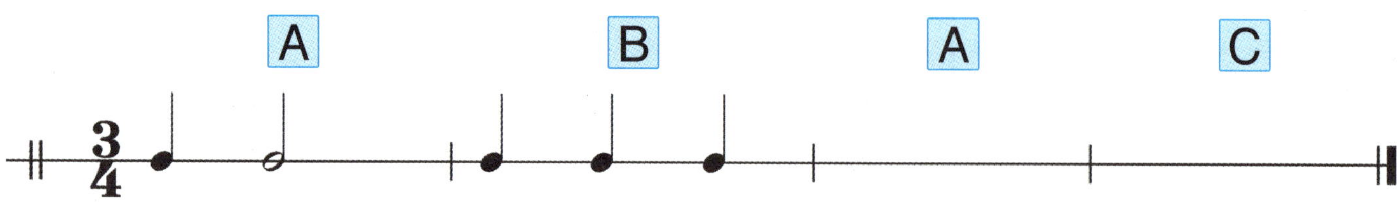

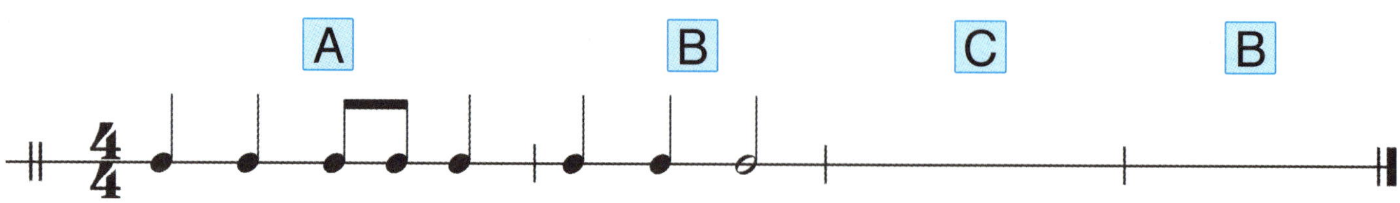

Assign with Lesson Book p.45

The Musical Private Eye

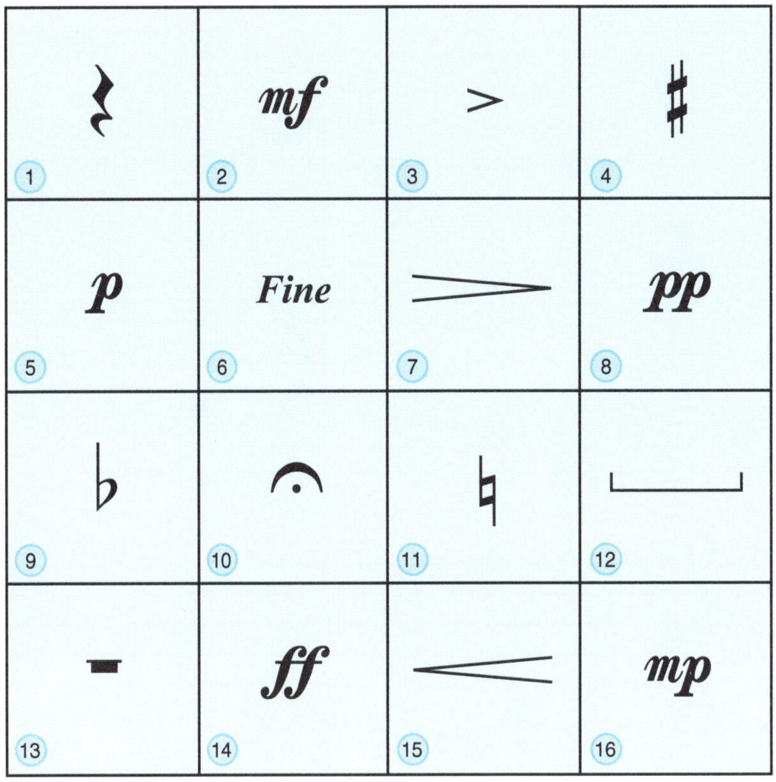

In the squares below, write the numbers that identify each musical clue given above.

QUARTER REST	1		PIANISSIMO (very soft)
NATURAL SIGN			FERMATA (hold sign)
FLAT SIGN			DIMINUENDO (gradually softer)
SHARP SIGN			CRESCENDO (gradually louder)
MEZZO PIANO (moderately soft)			PIANO (soft)
THE END			MEZZO FORTE (moderately loud)
WHOLE REST			PEDAL SIGN
ACCENT MARK			FORTISSIMO (very loud)

Add 10 points for each correct answer.
A perfect score is 150!

SCORE ________

Assign with Lesson Book p.46

Measuring 7ths

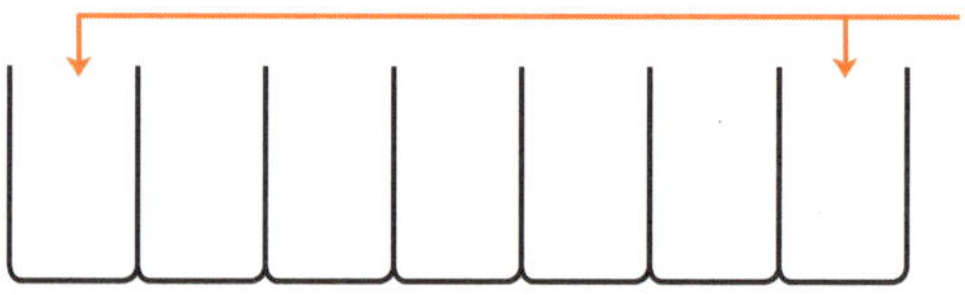

When you skip 5 white keys, the interval is a **7th.**

7ths are written LINE-LINE or SPACE-SPACE.

1. In each bar below, add a higher minim to make the indicated MELODIC interval.

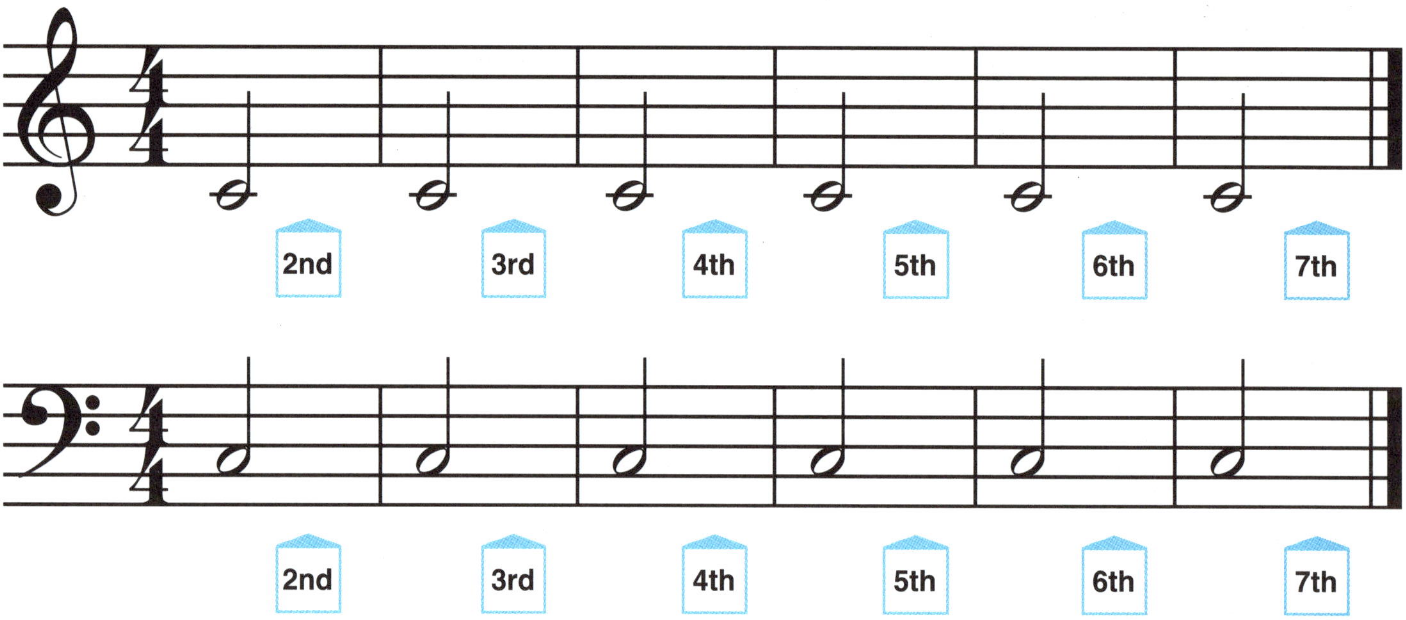

2. Play the above two lines. Use RH 1–5 or LH 5–1 on the 5th, 6th and 7th.

3. In each bar below, add a higher whole note to make HARMONIC 7th, as shown in the first example.

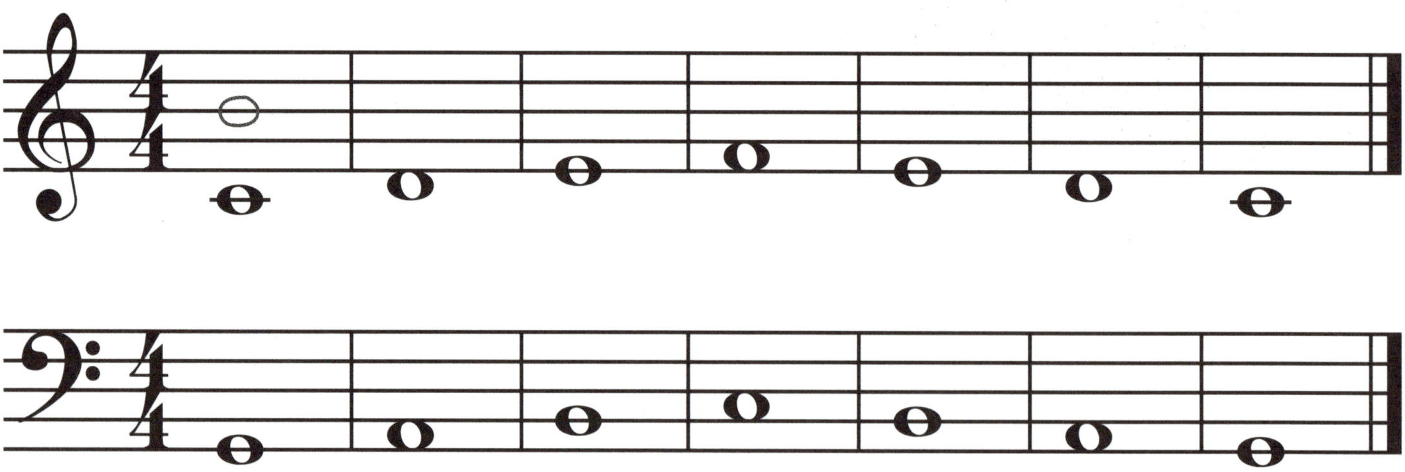

4. Play. Use RH $\frac{5}{1}$ or LH $\frac{1}{5}$ on each 7th.
   Students with hands too small to reach a 7th may divide each of the above lines between the hands, playing the bottom notes of the 7ths with LH 3, and the top notes with RH 3.

Writing the C Major Scale

1. Write the letter names of the notes of the C MAJOR SCALE, from *left to right,* on the keyboard below. Check each one with the TETRACHORD PATTERN as you write, to be sure the WHOLE TONES & SEMITONES are correct!

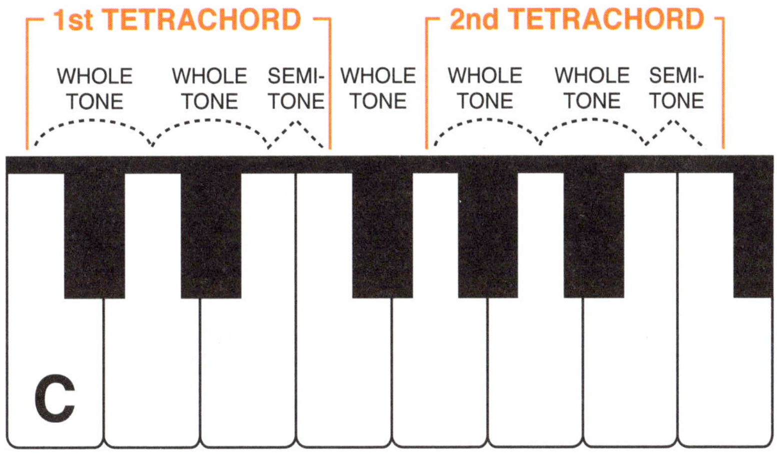

2. Complete the tetrachord beginning on C. Write one note over each finger number.

3. Complete the tetrachord beginning on G. Write one note over each finger number.

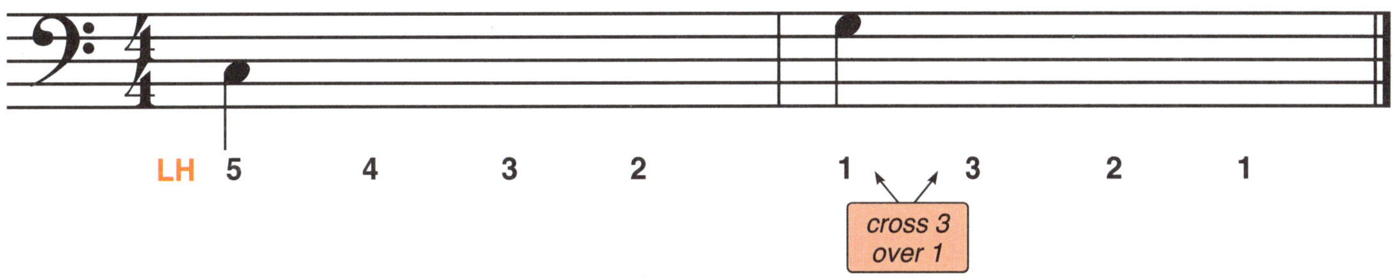

THIS IS THE COMPLETE C MAJOR SCALE, ASCENDING.

4. Play the C major scale with the LH, crossing 3 over 1.

5. Write the finger numbers over the notes of the following scale, starting with 5 and crossing 3 over 1.

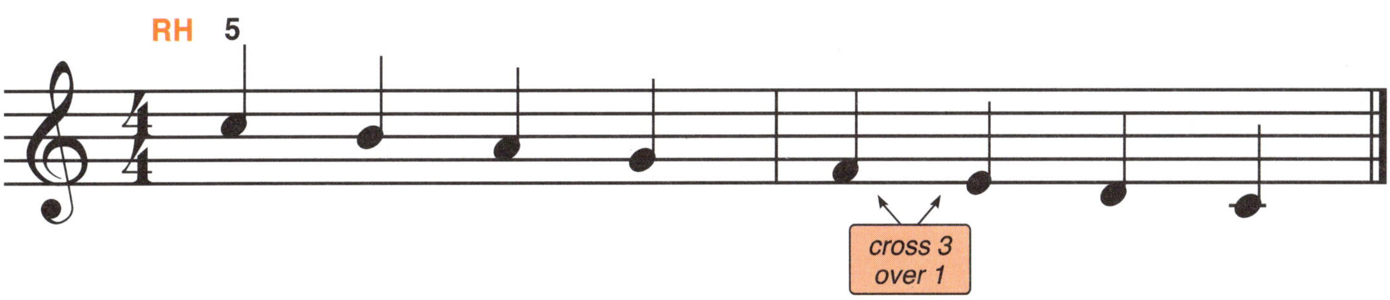

THIS IS THE COMPLETE C MAJOR SCALE, DESCENDING.

6. Play the C major scale with the RH, crossing 3 over 1.

Assign with Lesson Book p.56

Degrees of the Scale

Degrees of the scale are the successive notes that make up the scale. We number them in the same way we number intervals, but in this case it is the number of the note as it ascends the scale; like this:

SCALE OF C MAJOR

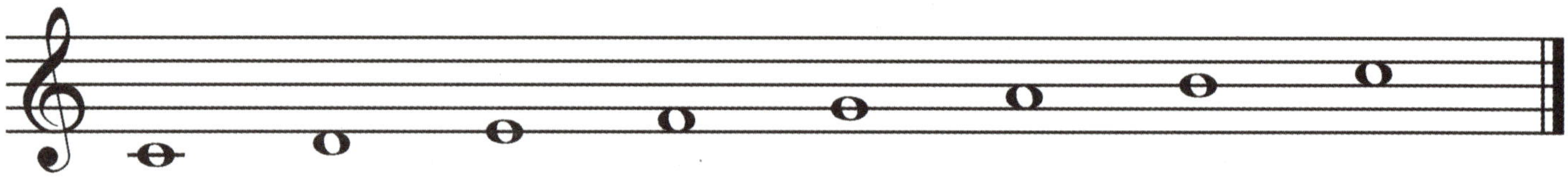

1. Fill in the note names for the following degrees of the C Major Scale:

Scale Degree	1st	2nd	3rd	4th	5th	6th	7th	1st
Note Name	C							

2. Finish writing the C Major Scale on the treble clef stave below, then fill in the boxes:

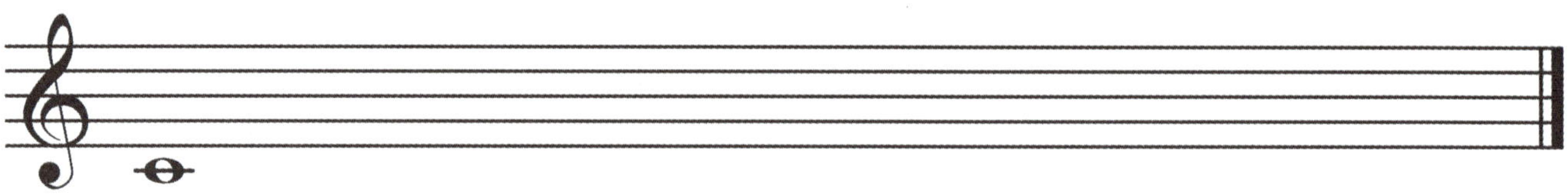

Note Name:			E		G		B	
Scale Degree:	1st	2nd				6th		

3. Finish writing the C Major Scale on the bass clef stave below, then fill in the boxes:

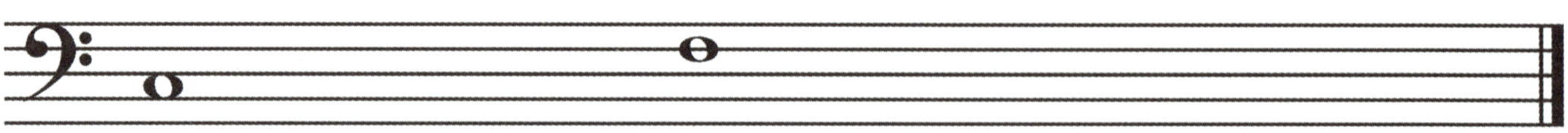

Note Name:	C					A		
Scale Degree:		2nd	3rd		5th		7th	

Review of the C Major Scale

A major scale consists of 8 notes. The first and last are the same and are called the keynote or **TONIC**. This note determines the KEY of the scale. The pattern for the major scale is:

Ascending:

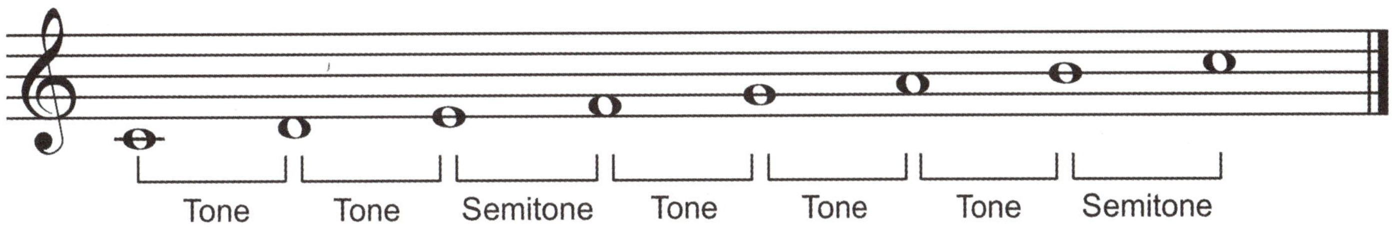

Descending:

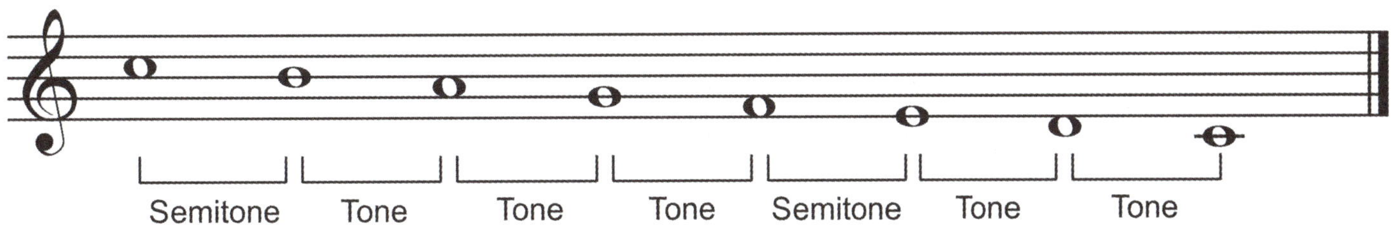

1. Write the letter names of the C major scale on the keyboard below:

2. Write the scale in semibreves (whole notes), marking the semitones with a bracket as above, but careful, this is in the bass clef!

Ascending:

Descending:

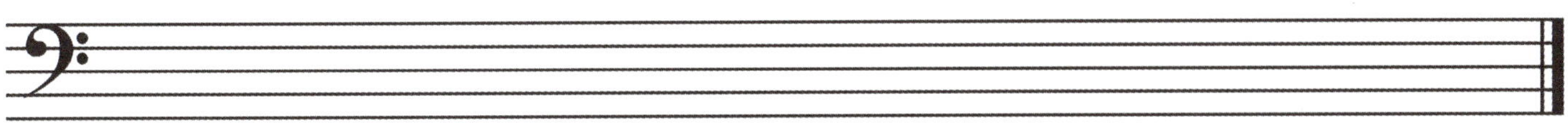

Assign with Lesson Book p.60

Writing Octaves

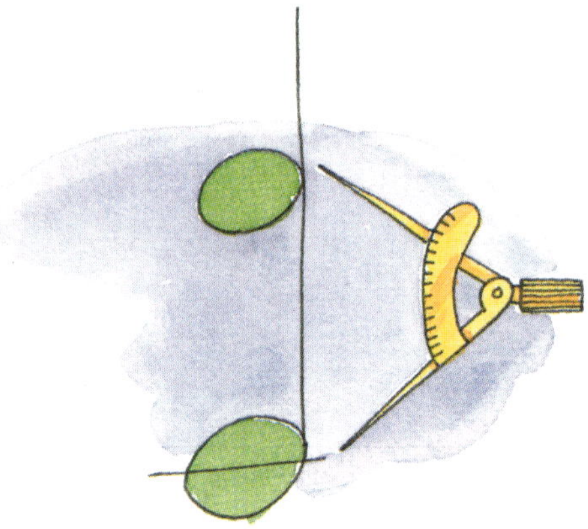

Remember: Octaves are written LINE-SPACE or SPACE-LINE.

1. In each bar below, add a higher minim to make the indicated MELODIC interval.

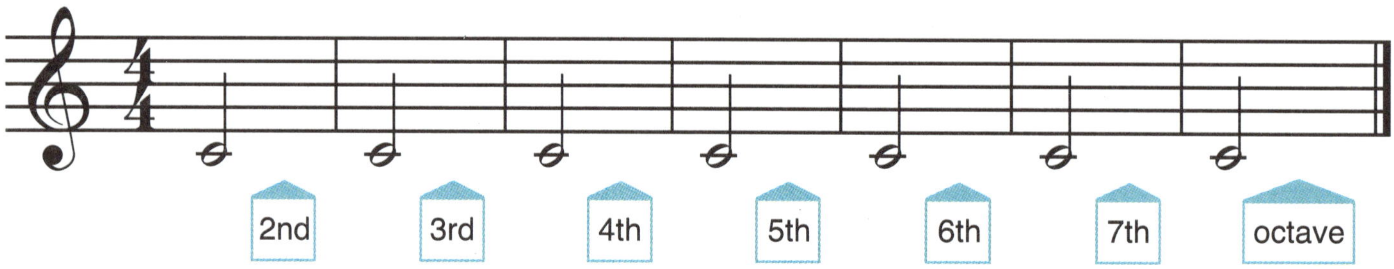

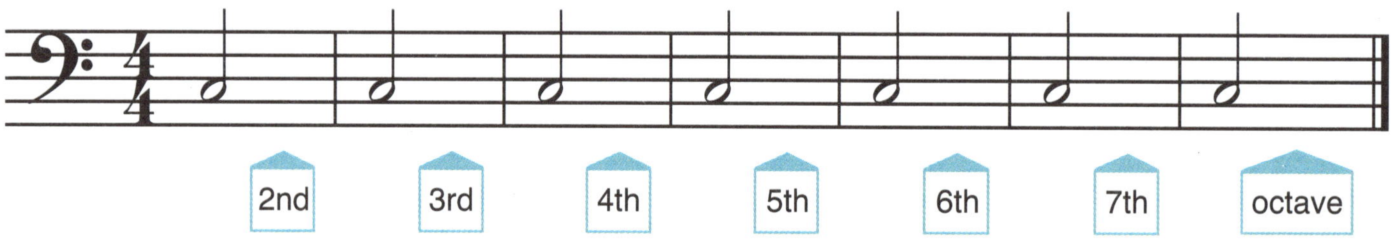

2. Play the above two lines. Use RH 1–5 on the 6th, 7th & octave. Use LH 5–1 on the 5th, 6th, 7th & octave.

3. Above each of the following notes write another semibreve to make a HARMONIC OCTAVE.

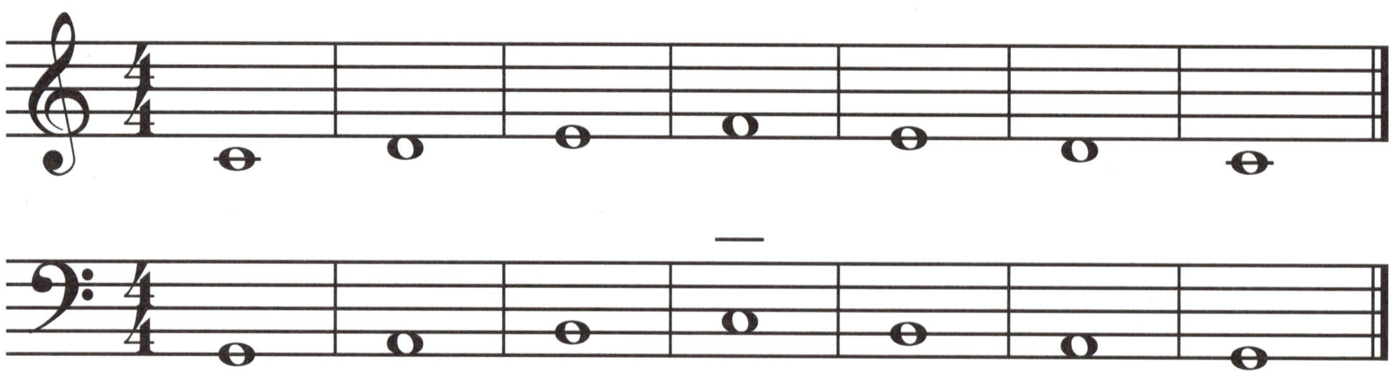

4. Play. Use RH 5–1 or LH 1–5 on each octave. Students with hands too small to reach an octave may divide each of the above lines between the hands, playing the bottom notes of the octaves with LH 3, and the top notes with RH 3.

Tips on Speed-Reading Intervals

EVEN numbered intervals
–2nds, 4ths, 6ths, octaves (8ths)–
have notes on
LINE-SPACE or SPACE-LINE.

ODD numbered intervals
–3rds, 5ths, 7ths–
have notes on
LINE-LINE or SPACE-SPACE.

See how quickly you can write the name of each interval in the box below it.

Use "2" for a 2nd, etc., and "8" for an OCTAVE.

EVEN NUMBERS (2nds, 4ths, 6ths, octaves)

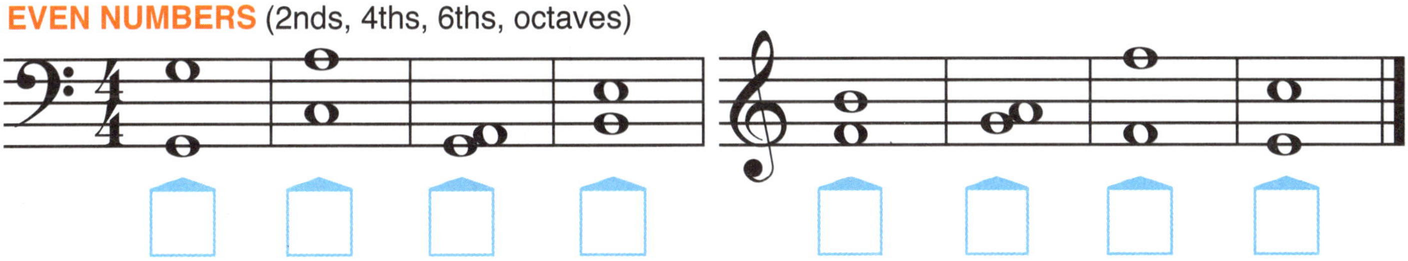

ODD NUMBERS (3rds, 5ths, 7ths)

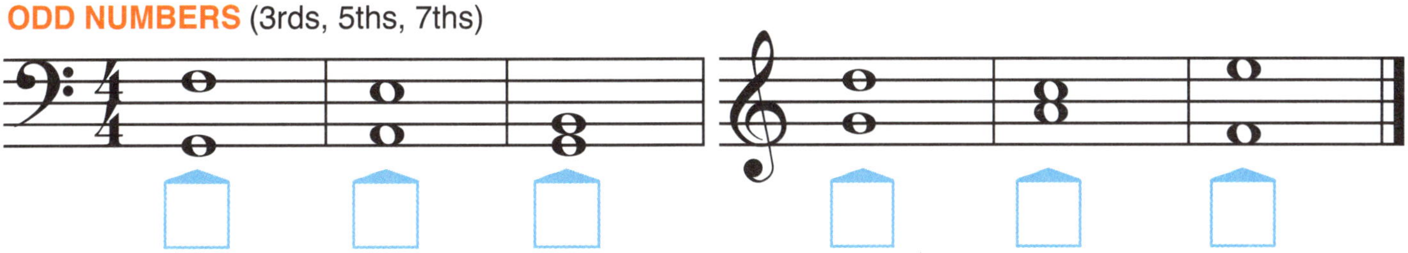

EVENS & ODDS

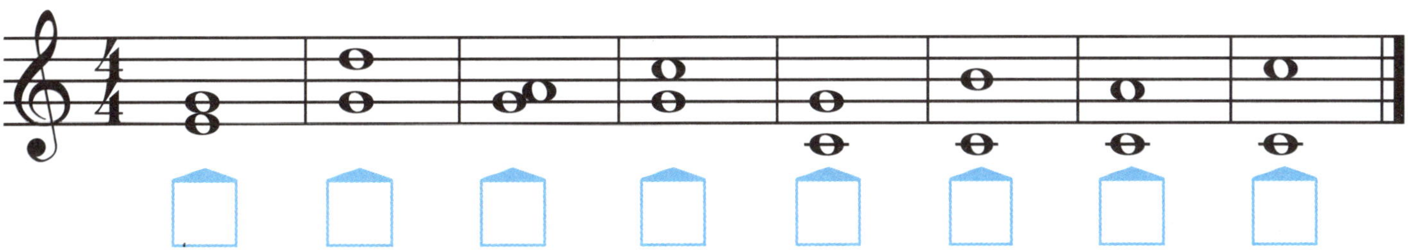

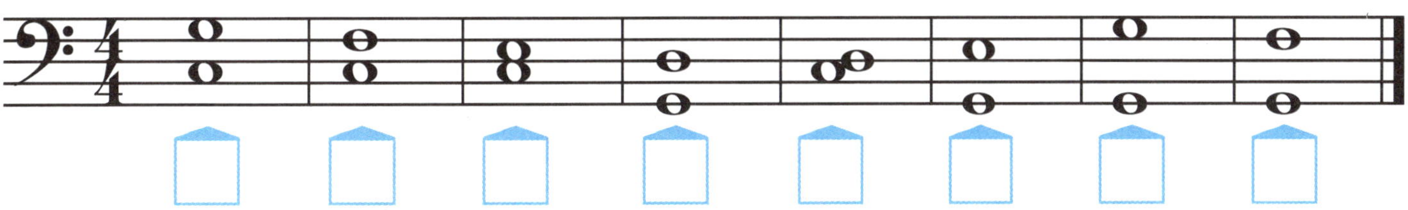

Assign with Lesson Book p.62

Crossing 3 over 1

to play the G MAJOR SCALE

1. Write the letter names of the notes of the G MAJOR SCALE, from *left to right*, on the keyboard below. Be sure the WHOLE TONES & SEMITONES are correct!

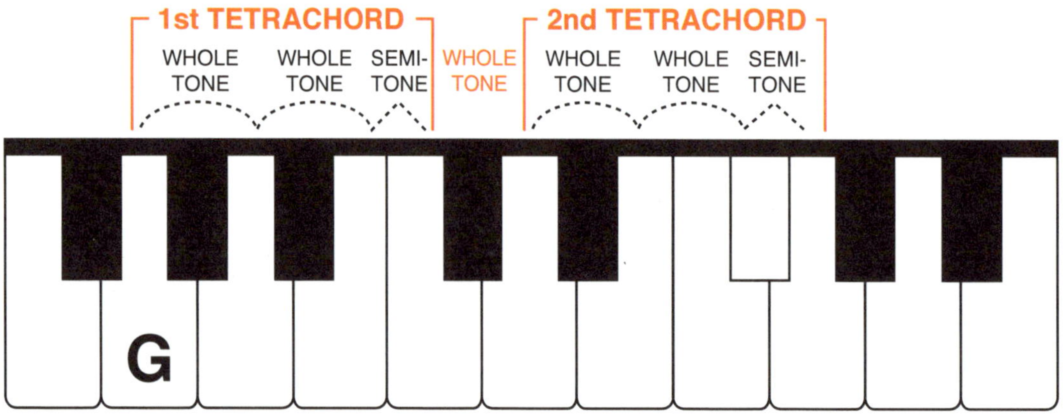

2. Complete the tetrachord beginning on G. Write one note over each finger number.

3. Complete the tetrachord beginning on D. Write one note over each finger number.

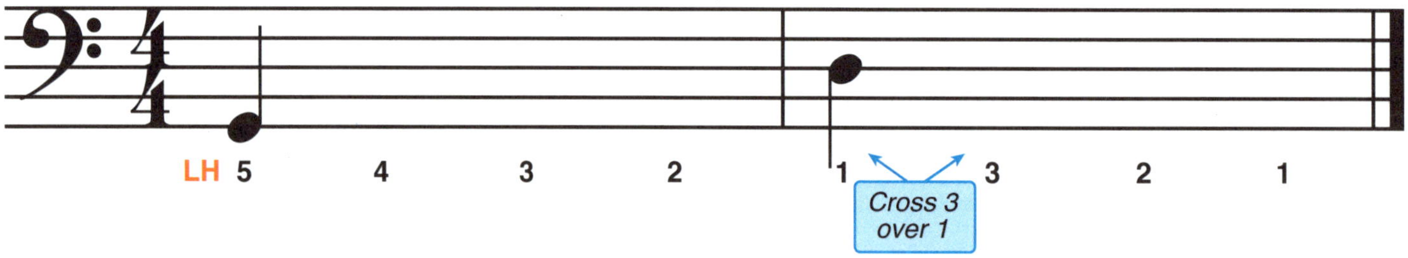

THIS IS THE COMPLETE G MAJOR SCALE, ASCENDING.

4. Play the G MAJOR SCALE with the LH, crossing 3 over 1.

5. Write the finger numbers over the notes of the following scale, starting with 5 and crossing 3 over 1.

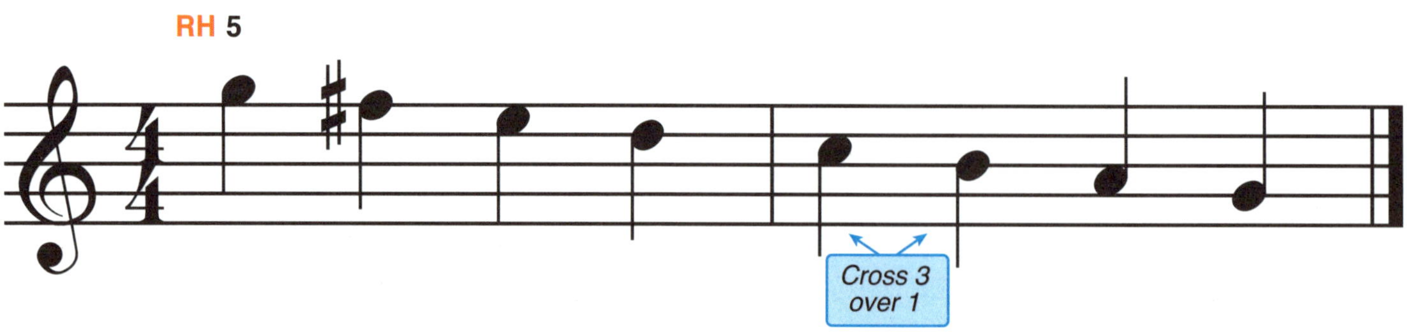

THIS IS THE COMPLETE G MAJOR SCALE, DESCENDING.

6. Play the G MAJOR SCALE with the RH, crossing 3 over 1.

Assign with Lesson Book p.62

Review of the G Major Scale

A major scale consists of 8 notes. The first and last are the same and are called the keynote or **TONIC**. This note determines the KEY of the scale. Do you remember the pattern for the major scale? (See p.23)

Now apply this pattern using G as the "keynote" (Tonic). Remember to bracket the tone and semitone intervals:

I've started you off...

Ascending:

Descending:

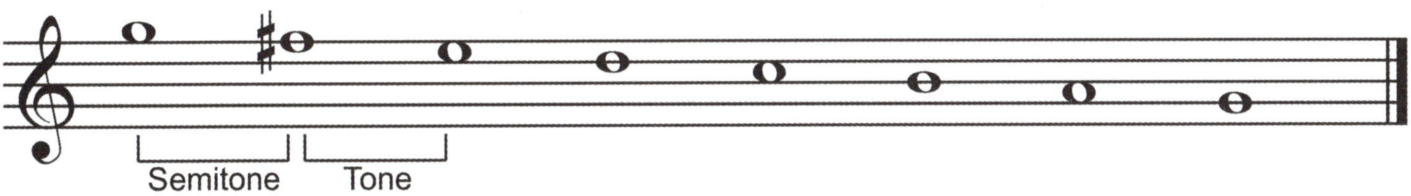

1. Write the letter names of the G major scale on the keyboard below:

Did you notice that to make the major scale pattern fit, we had to make every F an F♯? It would be very time consuming to write a ♯ before each F in a piece of music, so we simply add the sharp at the beginning of the piece. We call this the **KEY SIGNATURE**.

2. Write the scale in semibreves (whole notes), marking the tones and semitones with a bracket as above, but be careful, this is in the bass clef!

Ascending:

Descending:

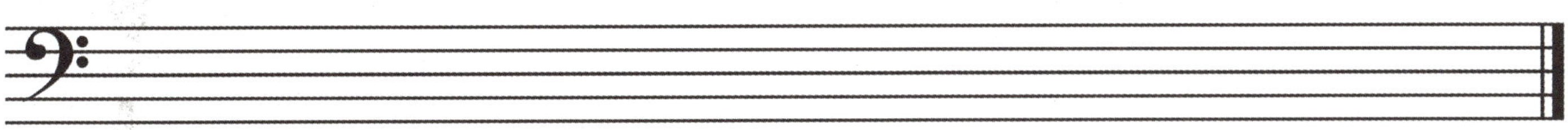

Assign with Lesson Book p.64

Theory Review

1. Complete these 4 bar rhythms:

a)

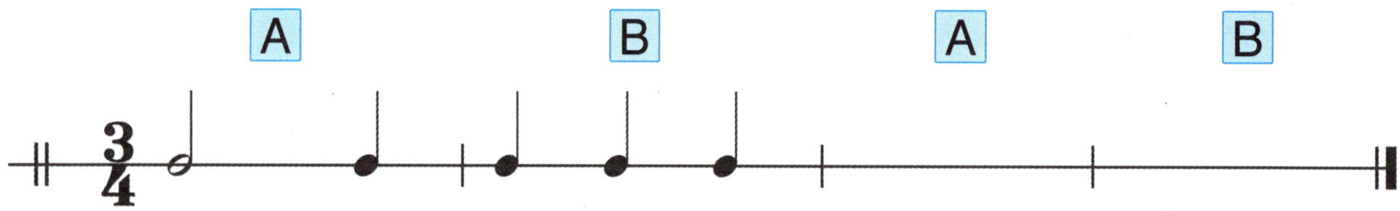

b)

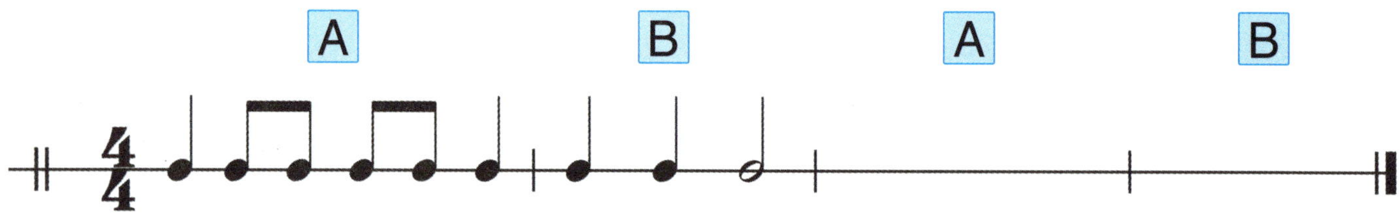

2. Write the dynamics ***p f mf ff mp pp*** in the correct order to create the effect described:

a) From very quiet to very loud:

b) From very loud to very quiet:

3. Write the scale degree of the notes with boxes below them:

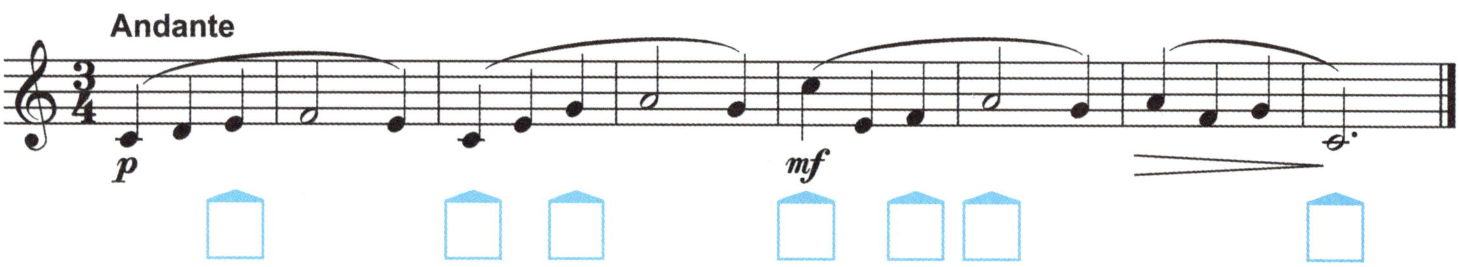

4. Rewrite these quaver (eighth note) rhythms with the correct beaming:

Unbeamed:

Beamed:

Alfred's Basic Graded Piano Course

UK Graded Exam Edition

Theory Book 2 • Preparatory

Theory

Willard A. Palmer • Morton Manus • Amanda Vick Lethco

Additional Pages: Andrew Higgins
Additional Artwork/Engraving: Oliver Wood
Additional Proofing: Leonie McCaughren
Cover Design: Holly Fraser

Produced by
Alfred Publishing Co. (UK) Ltd.
Burnt Mill, Elizabeth Way,
Harlow
Essex, CM20 2HX

alfreduk.com

ISBN-10: 1-4706-1310-7
ISBN-13: 978-1-4706-1310-5

Cover and Interior Illustrations by David Silverman (Painted by Cheryl Hennigar)